MAJESTIC HORSES

AMERICAN QUARTER HORSES

by Pamela Dell

Published in the United States of America by The Child's World®
PO Box 326 • Chanhassen, MN 55317-0326
800-599-READ • www.childsworld.com

PHOTO CREDITS
© Arco Images/Alamy
© Bettmann/Corbis: 16
© Dale C. Spartas/Corbis: 7
© Frank Lukasseck/zefa/Corbis: 4, 25
© iStockphoto.com/ImagesbyTrista: 21
© iStockphoto.com/WorldWideImages: 19
© Jack Fields/Corbis: 23
© Juniors Bildarchiv/Alamy: cover, 1
© Lothar Lenz/zefa/Corbis: 11
© Mark J. Barrett/Alamy: 8
© Russ Merne/Alamy: 26
© The Granger Collection, New York: 12

ACKNOWLEDGMENTS
The Child's World®: Mary Berendes, Publishing Director;
Katherine Stevenson, Editor

Content Adviser: Weezee

The Design Lab: Kathleen Petelinsek, Design and Page Production

LIBRARY OF CONGRESS CATALOGING-IN-PUBLICATION DATA
Dell, Pamela.
  American quarter horses / by Pamela Dell.
     p. cm. — (Majestic horses)
  Includes bibliographical references and index.
  ISBN 1-59296-779-5 (library bound: alk. paper)
  1. Quarter horse—Juvenile literature. I. Title. II. Series.
  SF293.Q3D35 2007
  636.1'33—dc22
                                              2006022642

TABLE OF CONTENTS

HARD-WORKING HORSES

The little calf squeals. A minute ago, it was running beside its mother. It was part of a big herd. But now, a fast, powerful horse is running towards it. The calf will be easy to catch.

The rancher on the horse's back rides easily in the saddle. The horse knows just what to do. It moves the calf away from the herd. Now the rancher can rope the calf and **brand** it. Then the calf can return to the herd. The horse keeps working until all the calves are branded. Only one **breed** of horse could do this job so well—the American quarter horse.

Quarter horses can start, stop, and turn quickly. They are very fast over short distances.

Have you been to a rodeo? Have you watched Western movies? If so, you have seen American quarter horses!

◄ This rancher is riding a quarter horse. The rope is used for catching cattle.

WHAT DO QUARTER HORSES LOOK LIKE?

American quarter horses are sturdy, power-packed animals. They are famous for their quick, sudden getaways. You can see the strength in their bodies. Their chests are large. Their legs are short but sturdy.

Quarter horses are not the tallest of breeds. A horse's height is measured at the **withers**. Most quarter horses are 58 to 63 inches (147 to 160 centimeters) tall. They are often heavy for their size. Most of them weigh 900 to 1,200 pounds (410 to 540 kilograms).

A horse's height is also measured in *hands*. A hand is 4 inches (10 centimeters). Most quarter horses stand 14 to 15 hands high.

This quarter horse is enjoying a sunny day. You can see how powerful its body is. ▶

Quarter horses are built differently for different kinds of jobs. Those raised for working cattle tend to be shorter and stockier. Those raised for racing tend to be taller and thinner.

Quarter horses almost always come in solid colors. Most of them are **chestnut**, **bay**, or other colors of brown. But they come in other colors, too. Some are **palomino**, **roan**, gray, or black. The gray ones are so light that many people call them white. Some quarter horses have white markings on their faces or lower legs.

◀ Here you can see lots of quarter-horse colors. Quarter horses with large patches of white on their bodies are called *paints*.

NEWBORN QUARTER HORSES

Newborn **foals** have a thick, fuzzy coat. The extra hair keeps them warm. The hair thins out when the weather warms. The foal's coat becomes smooth and shiny, like its parents'.

Many foals are around people right away. If they are handled gently, they learn to trust people quickly. That makes them easy to handle later on. Some foals, though, are not around people very much. It can take them longer to trust people. After a few months, ranch hands round up the horses. Then the foals can start learning to trust people.

Some foals change color as they grow older. A dark foal might turn out to be light gray.

This quarter-horse foal is lying in a grassy field. The white mark on its face is called a *blaze*. ▶

QUARTER HORSES IN HISTORY

North America had no horses when Europeans arrived. Some of the Europeans' horses got loose. Native Americans caught them and began raising their own horses.

Quarter horses are an American breed. They came from a mix of other breeds. European settlers brought horses from Spain, England, and other countries. They began mixing their different kinds of horses. They mixed them with Native Americans' horses, too. They were trying to make faster, stronger horses.

American settlers were already racing horses by the middle 1600s. In the Southeast, the races were short, fast **sprints**. They were only about one-quarter mile (four-tenths of a kilometer) long. Most of these races were not on racetracks. They were on roads—or even just patches of open ground.

◀ This painting shows Spanish explorers in 1540. Some of the horses from this group, (and other explorers' groups) got loose. Those horses are relatives of today's quarter horses.

Settlers wanted horses that could do well in these short races. They chose parents that were fast and strong. Some of the parents were English Thoroughbreds. Others were horses raised by the Chickasaw and Choctaw tribes. The racehorses got faster. The fastest were called **Celebrated** American Quarter Running Horses.

As settlers moved west, their quarter-mile horses went with them. The settlers kept mixing these horses with other kinds. The horses got even better. They seemed made for the West. They could run fast and make quick turns. They had no problem with hilly, rocky country.

Why did quarter horses get that name? Because they are so fast at running one-quarter mile. It takes them only about 20 seconds.

This quarter horse has the palomino coloring. Palominos have golden-brown bodies and light manes and tails. ▶

Lots of people in the West raised cattle. They needed horses for rounding up and working with these animals.

In 1940, the breed got its modern name—the American Quarter Horse.

They needed horses that could stop, start, and turn fast. They needed horses that could work well under any conditions. Quarter horses were the perfect choice! Soon they were found throughout the West. In the 1900s, people started to use cars and trucks. But they still used quarter horses for lots of ranch work.

In 1940, people started keeping track of quarter-horse families. They kept track of which horses had babies. They wrote down the names of each horse's parents and grandparents. People still do that today.

◀ This painting shows someone roping a steer. Quarter horses were great for this job!

WHAT ARE QUARTER HORSES LIKE?

A quarter horse can be a rancher's best friend! Life on a ranch is not easy. But quarter horses do not seem to mind. They work hard when they have a job to do. Other horses might give up—but not quarter horses.

Quarter horses are steady and sure-footed, too. This makes them good riding horses. Hard trails do not bother them. They are also easy to work with. They are gentle and easygoing. They do not get upset without a good reason. Once they get to know you, quarter horses are true friends. That makes them great family pets, too.

Quarter horses' calmness makes them good choices for kids. Lots of kids ride and show quarter horses.

This rancher is spinning a rope to make a *lasso*. A lasso works well for catching cattle. ▶

QUARTER HORSES AT WORK

Today, American quarter horses are used for all kinds of riding. Many people ride them just for fun. They enjoy riding them on trails or cross-country. Quarter horses do well at jumping and in horse shows, too.

Even today, no horse breed is better at working with cattle! Quarter horses are said to have "cow sense." Working with cattle is not easy. But these horses seem to know how—even with little training. They are still used for ranch work. They are **popular** for rodeos, too. And they take part in Western-style races and **contests**. They are great at barrel racing, roping, herding, and cutting.

"Cutting" is a ranching word. It means getting a cow to move away from the herd.

This barrel racer is leaning into a turn. Barrel racing is fast and fun! ▶

Quarter horses started out racing, and they still race today. They still run in the sprints that gave them their name. In the 1800s, Thoroughbred racing became more popular. People lost interest in quarter racing. But today, quarter racing is big again. On a short track, watch out! American quarter horses still leave other breeds in the dust.

Quarter horses are good at cross-country racing, too. Some of these races are very long. The horses go 25 to 100 miles (40 to 161 kilometers) in a single day. Some of the races go on for days. The horses must be strong and in good shape.

Quarter horses can reach speeds of 55 miles (88 kilometers) an hour! They are the fastest breed over a short distance.

These quarter horses are racing toward the finish line. The riders crouch down to help them go faster. ▶

★·★ AMERICAN QUARTER HORSES TODAY

Americans love quarter horses! In fact, the U.S. alone has over 4 million of them. They are one of the nation's most popular breeds. They are popular in other places, too—and there are more all the time. Their numbers are growing in Mexico, Japan, Israel, Italy, England, and Wales. People in Brazil and Australia are raising quarter horses, too. Quarter horses do well on these countries' huge ranches.

Many areas have clubs for quarter-horse owners. They help the owners keep up with all the latest news.

This quarter horse is running in an Oregon field. ▶

People sometimes talk about "stopping on a dime and turning on a penny." Stopping on a dime means running fast and stopping quickly. Turning on a penny means turning fast. For American quarter horses, nothing could be easier!

These horses have played a big part in North American history. And they are a big part of the horse world today. They are good at all kinds of jobs. And they are lots fun to ride!

Quarter horses are popular in movies and on TV. In fact, they show up more than any other breed.

◄ This quarter horse has the chestnut coloring. It lives on a farm in Alberta, Canada.

★ ★ ★ BODY PARTS OF A HORSE

1. Ears
2. Forelock
3. Forehead
4. Eyes
5. Nostril
6. Lips
7. Muzzle
8. Chin
9. Cheek
10. Neck
11. Shoulder
12. Chest
13. Forearm
14. Knee
15. Cannon
16. Coronet
17. Hoof

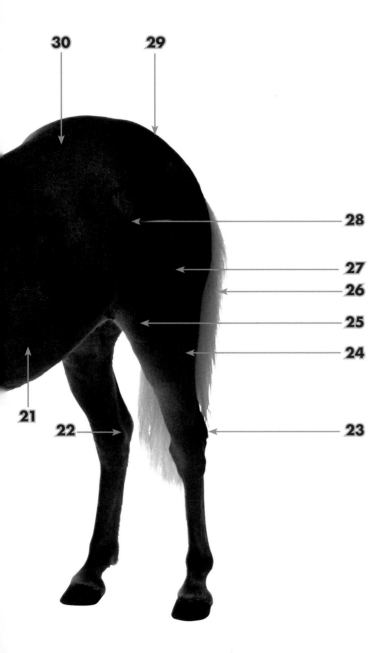

18. Pastern
19. Fetlock
20. Elbow
21. Barrel
22. Chestnut
23. Hock
24. Gaskin
25. Stifle
26. Tail
27. Thigh
28. Point of hip
29. Croup
30. Loin
31. Back
32. Withers
33. Mane
34. Poll

GLOSSARY

bay (BAY) A bay horse is brown with a black mane and tail. Many quarter horses are bays.

brand (BRAND) To brand an animal is to put an owner's mark on it. Quarter horses help ranchers brand cattle.

breed (BREED) A breed is a certain type of an animal. American quarter horses are a well-known breed.

celebrated (SEH-luh-bray-ted) If something is celebrated, it is talked about and widely known. People called early quarter-mile racehorses "celebrated."

chestnut (CHEST-nut) A chestnut horse is reddish brown with a brown mane and tail. Many quarter horses are chestnuts.

contests (KAHN-tests) In contests, people or animals try to win by being the best at something. Quarter horses are good at many kinds of contests.

foals (FOHLZ) Foals are baby horses. Quarter-horse foals can learn to trust people quickly.

palomino (PA-luh-MEE-noh) Palomino horses are a golden color with a light mane and tale. Some quarter horses are palominos.

popular (PAH-pyuh-lur) When something is popular, it is liked by lots of people. Quarter horses are very popular.

roan (ROHN) Roan horses are a solid color with a few white hairs. Some quarter horses are roans.

sprints (SPRINTS) Sprints are short, high-speed races. Quarter horses are great sprinters.

withers (WIH-thurz) The withers is the highest part of a horse's back. A quarter horse's height is measured at the withers.

TO FIND OUT MORE

In the Library

Funston, Sylvia. *The Kids' Horse Book*. Toronto: Maple Tree Press, 1993.

Patent, Dorothy Hinshaw, and William Muñoz (photographer). *Quarter Horses*. New York: Holiday House, 1985.

Price, Steven D. *The Kids' Book of the American Quarter Horse*. New York: Lyons Press, 1999.

Ransford, Sandy. *The Kingfisher Illustrated Horse & Pony Encyclopedia*. New York: Kingfisher, 2004.

On the Web

Visit our Web site for lots of links about American quarter horses: *http://www.childsworld.com/links*

Note to Parents, Teachers, and Librarians: We routinely check our Web links to make sure they're safe, active sites—so encourage your readers to check them out!

31

INDEX

About the author: Pamela Dell is the author of more than fifty books for young people. She likes writing about four-legged animals as well as insects, birds, famous people, and interesting times in history. She has published both fiction and nonfiction books and has also created several interactive computer games for kids. Pamela divides her time between Los Angeles, where the weather is mostly warm and sunny all year, and Chicago, where she loves how wildly the seasons change every few months.